DON'T BE AN ASS

DON'T BE AN ASS

9 Mistakes Guaranteed to Destroy Any Relationship

MARK GUNGOR DIANE BRAY
Illustrations by **Johnathan Brown**

DON'T BE AN ASS

DON'T BE AN ASS
9 Mistakes Guaranteed to Destroy Any Relationship

By MARK GUNGOR and DIANE BRAY
Illustrations by Johnathan Brown
Book design by Debbie Bishop

Special thanks to Joe Grier and Larry Patterson for contributing their time and effort to the writing of this book.

Copyright 2016 Mark Gungor, All Rights Reserved.
All rights reserved, including the right to reproduce this book or portions thereof in any form whatsoever.

Scripture quotations taken from The Holy Bible, New International Version [R] NIV [R] Copyright [C] 1973, 1978, 1984, 2011 by Biblica, Inc. [TM] Used by permission. All rights reserved worldwide.

Printed in China

For information address inquiries to: info@laughyourway.com

To Ezra...

CONTENTS

Introduction ii

Chapter 1 - Don't Be a Jack Ass 1

Chapter 2 - Don't Be a Lazy Ass 9

Chapter 3 - Don't Be a Hard Ass 19

Chapter 4 - Don't Be a Dumb Ass 27

Chapter 5 - Don't Be a Smart Ass 37

Chapter 6 - Don't Be a Bad Ass 45

Chapter 7 - Don't Be a Cheap Ass 53

Chapter 8 - Don't Be a Whiney Ass 63

Chapter 9 - Don't Be a Crazy Ass 71

Conclusion 78

DON'T BE AN ASS

INTRODUCTION

Ok – let's start with the big question on everyone's mind...

"Why would you use such a crass word for a relationship book?! I thought you were a pastor!!"

Well, first of all, who says this is a crass word? Who, exactly, did we ever install in the great world of Christendom as the official Word Police?? I don't ever remember voting on that issue. And secondly, direct and stark talk is exactly what a lot of people need. Besides, it is *totally* acceptable to use crass words and analogies to make points. How do I know that? Because we actually see it in the Bible.

But let's start with the debate over the word itself. The word ass is used 86 times in 76 verses in the King James Bible. So clearly, the word can be used. "But they were talking about donkeys!!" Yes...and what were *you* thinking?? Take a look at the illustrations in this book: They are of donkeys – not derrières.

And besides, the Bible *does* use some crass words and

analogies. The Apostle Paul was the greatest offender.

> *What is more, I consider everything a loss because of the surpassing worth of knowing Christ Jesus my Lord, for whose sake I have lost all things. I consider them garbage, that I may gain Christ. – Philippians 3:8 NIV*

Garbage?? That is a bit of a light translation. Older versions use words like "dung". And many scholars believe Paul used the commonly crude term of the day. In other words, he *literally* said that he counted all of his former accomplishments a big pile of sh*t. Doubt me? Ask your pastor...

And let us not forget the crass analogy Paul used when writing to the Galatians who were insisting that all Christian men should be circumcised.

> *As for those agitators, I wish they would go the whole way and emasculate themselves! – Galatians 5:12 NIV*

He *literally* said he wished that the guys who advocated for circumcision would go the whole way and cut their wieners off entirely!! A bit crass, to say the least. So, don't get too excited about the use of the word *ass*.

"But why use such a word??!!"

Because, quite frankly, no other word more clearly and succinctly defines the attributes I am talking about. And despite how *holy* you think you are, you and everyone else in the English-speaking world knows *exactly* what these phrases mean.

I have on more than one occasion, dealt with someone experiencing the negative consequences of some stupid thing they had said or done to their spouse. They always ask with desperation the inevitable question, "What should I do?" My answer is always the same: "Don't be an ass!"

This is not rocket science! When you treat someone badly you are going to get bad results.

When you are intolerable, an obnoxious boar, an insensitive mocking fool, an impatient and demanding overlord – just what exactly do you *think* is going to happen??

And consider all those adjectives I just used; most offenders

> This is not rocket science! When you treat someone badly you are going to get bad results.

would never comprehend or properly respond to any of those statements. We can try to communicate to the offender in the most appropriate, sincere, spiritually sensitive and Focus on the Family approved terminology, but at the end of the day there is only one universally accepted phrase that virtually *everybody* understands: Don't be an ass!

In my former book, *The Be Attitudes of Marriage*, I proffered that the key to any successful relationship can be summed up in two very simple words: Be nice. But sometimes concepts can be more clearly communicated when viewed from a negative perspective. For example: We can tell people that smoking may have a negative impact on their well being and may possibly result in symptoms like shortness of breath and that smoking has the potential to rob them of the full energy and zest that life has to offer. That would be the positive approach. But the strongest argument is actually made from a negative point of view: Smoking will kill you.

> ...there is only one universally accepted phrase that virtually *everybody* understands: Don't be an ass!

So while I have advocated from a positive perspective that people just "Be nice" to each other, I now offer, in this writing, an approach that perhaps even more may understand: Don't be an ass.

DON'T BE AN ASS

CHAPTER 1:
Don't Be a Jack Ass
(AKA a Stubborn Ass) (AKA Horse's Ass)

Someone who won't listen. One who is unrepentant and unyielding.

What comes to mind when you think of a mule, AKA jackass?

A stubborn animal that won't cooperate is how most people would describe said creature. And so it is with people. You want to harm any relationship you are in? Act like the typical Jack Ass. Refuse to listen to everyone around you. Don't take any advice. Shun wisdom that others speak into your life. Insist upon your own way…at all or most times and at all cost. Never apologize. Never take responsibility for your actions. It's the perfect recipe for burning bridges and destroying your relationships. (Which is probably why you are reading this book!)

The adage, "It's my way or the highway" is among the favorite modus operandi of Jack Asses. The problem is, it doesn't get them very far down the road when it comes to matters of relationships. They might actually even ask for your opinion or inquire what you think or want…but alas, true Jack Asses will then refute and debate every

DON'T BE AN ASS

facet of your idea. They will bull-headedly explain why it won't work, why it's not possible, why you are wrong. Until, out of frustration and exhaustion, you give up. It can be anything as simple as what color to paint the walls in the bathroom or the best way to light a campfire, all the way to financial planning decisions or the best way to discipline children.

Look, no one knows everything. Yet, there are those among us who act as if they do. They are the armchair quarterbacks of life, frequently offering opinion, advice, and contradiction on a wide variety of topics they have no involvement or expertise in. You can't tell them anything about anything. They know it all.

And since they are like Carnac the Magnificent (I am showing my age for those of you who don't remember the Johnny Carson character) and know all the answers, they consistently believe themselves to be right. After all, they couldn't possibly be *wrong* anywhere in their vast array of incomparable brainpower and knowledge.

Listen, Jack Ass! Don't be ridiculous. EVERYONE is wrong about something at some point. Generally speaking, we are often wrong about a great many things at a great many points in life.

Let's face it. If any one of us could live a perfect and spotless life where we were never wrong, we'd be sinless and then we'd be....

Oh yeah, that's right...we'd be Jesus! Last time I checked there was only one Lord and Savior who is perfect and it's not you or me!

Proverbs 12:15 nails it when saying, *"The way of fools seems right to them, but the wise listen to advice."* And Solomon continued with: *"Do you see a person wise in their own eyes? There is more hope for a fool than for them."* (Proverbs 26:12)

> "The problem with people who are always right and never wrong is that they see no reason to learn the words: I'm sorry."

The problem with people who are *always* right and *never* wrong, is that they see no reason to learn the words: *I'm sorry.* No matter that in reality they are incorrect in their behaviors, for Jack Asses are so resistant to any other opinions or advice, so unrepentant and unswerving in their belief that they are right and the rest of the world is wrong, so unyielding in their paths are they, that they have absolutely convinced themselves I AM RIGHT. They will fight to the death...or at least to the death of the relationship...to prove their point.

He can be 75 minutes late for a dinner reservation, or forget your anniversary; she can insult you wildly in front of your co-workers

DON'T BE AN ASS

at a party or totally undermine a decision you made regarding your teenager's curfew, yet when you challenge, question, or call them out on it, there is no way they will own it, nor offer any concession.

And if, God forbid, they actually catch a glimmer of truth and fact, and consider they just *might* possibly be wrong, there is still no room for apology. A dyed in the wool Jack Ass will *still* not offer any form of mea culpa! They will only make excuses or find some loophole or discover a way to blame someone else: "*You* are being overly sensitive. *You* misunderstood. *You* didn't ask me. *You* didn't remind me. *You* didn't interpret the facts correctly. *You* are trying to control everything. The moon wasn't full, and the stars weren't in perfect alignment and the trade winds were blowing in a more northerly direction." Whatever excuse or justification works for the infraction.

And, in typical Jack Ass behavior, when truly backed into a corner and confronted with their error, they resort to their favorite escape clause: *I never said that.* Ever have someone change their story once they are called out? Rather than admitting fault, so strong is the need to never back down, that they will switch course and insist that they never said or did something that you could swear on a stack of Bibles you witnessed. (Which by the way, you aren't supposed to do.)

Stubborn pride never allows for apology or repentance. But pride also leads to the undoing of a person, and most certainly, the undoing of relationships. Scripture tells us in Proverbs 16:18 that, *"Pride goes before destruction, a haughty spirit before a fall."* When you are so entrenched in your own thoughts, opinions and ideas, that you have no room to consider that maybe, *just maybe*, you are not 100% right, 100% of the time, you have issues. Pride issues. And *your* issues are the cause of relational issues with your kids, your spouse, your boss and probably every person you know. Proverbs 13:10 explains to us, *"Where there is strife, there is pride, but wisdom is found in those who take advice."* Yet, most Jack Asses don't see it as *their* problem. The source of the strife could not possibly be *them*. They point fingers, assign blame and cast aspersions on anyone they can. They are fools and only a fool seeks his own way, rather than gaining wisdom.

     Don't be a Jack Ass. Don't jeopardize your relationships, your marriage, your job. Let go of your stubborn pride before disgrace comes— assuming that most Jack Asses reading this haven't already experienced some grave fall or level of disgrace—and

> " Stubborn pride never allows for apology or repentance. "

DON'T BE AN ASS

get some humility. Gain wisdom. Again from Proverbs, the Book of Wisdom: *When pride comes, then comes disgrace, but with humility, comes wisdom.* (Proverbs 11:12)

It takes real humility to seek wisdom and to admit one's faults and shortcomings. For some, to offer apology is the equivalent of lopping off their left leg (or some other equally important body part) and they absolutely will never give utterance to the words, "I'm sorry. I was wrong. Please forgive me."

For those of us well versed in words of confession and amends, it seems ludicrous and beyond comprehension as to *why* others just can't seem to eek out the teeniest of apologies. When "I'm sorry" and "I was wrong" are main staples in one's vocabulary, there is no way to grasp the fact that another person simply cannot or will not cough up words of concession. So what gives?

For some, apology or admitting fault or error feels like a sign of great weakness. Little do they understand that it is actually a show of strength, not surrender and capitulation. Acting as a know-it-all, I-never-back-down, you-can't-tell-me-what-to-do Jack Ass is the counterfeit way of demonstrating might on the outside, when in all probability, what they feel on the inside is incompetent, inept and inadequate. But only *they* have the power to wrestle with and come to grips with their own insecurities.

If you are seeing a reflection of yourself in this description, do yourself and everyone around you a favor...especially those who love you - tackle the tough job of getting free from your self-doubt. Get comfortable with yourself so you can let go of the bloviating swagger and ditch the mask you are hiding behind at the expense of your relationships.

Learn to accept advice. Grow in your wisdom—not just knowledge. The prideful fool may have a lot of knowledge, but not yet have gained a whole lot of wisdom. Knowledge puffs up, but *wisdom* says, "You were right, I was wrong – I'm sorry."

Get comfortable with those eight little words. They have the power to change any relationship. Being able to voice them will save you countless hours of heartache and arguments.

They might even save your marriage.

> It takes real humility to seek wisdom and to admit one's faults and shortcomings.

DON'T BE AN ASS

CHAPTER 2:
Don't Be a Lazy Ass
(AKA a Half Ass)

Someone who won't follow through. One who talks big, but takes no action, is lazy and shows no commitment.

> **Merriam-Webster Dictionary defines lazy as "averse or disinclined to work, activity, or exertion."**

Surprisingly, the word half-assed is also in there (You see? Not too crass for Webster!) and is defined as "lacking significance, adequacy, character, completeness or effectiveness." And boy, oh, boy, if that doesn't describe a whole sector of our culture today. Sadly, (and most unfortunately) it is becoming an increasing portion of our population.

There was a time when only a small fraction of our society could be termed as lazy or uncommitted to their family, work, faith and relationships. NOW, it seems as if the ratio has nearly flipped. Far too many people in recent generations have a tendency to be Lazy Asses at worst, and Half Asses at best. Granted, part of this trend of reversal has much of its roots in the changes in our culture. We are no longer a primarily agrarian society. Hard work and labor on family farms where

DON'T BE AN ASS

"if you-don't-work, you-don't-eat" has been replaced with sedentary jobs that often guarantee a "lunch in spite of what you do here" ethic.

Consider, also, the many forms of entertainment (frequently conducive to sloth) that have appeared on the scene in the past thirty years. When I was growing up in Neillsville, Wisconsin, there were only three channels: ABC, CBS and NBC – though most people could only get two of them, unless you had a big antenna that you could rotate to ABC out of La Crosse. Today, I have hundreds of channels being pumped into my living room on a large, flat screen High Definition TV. (Well, actually my living room, my bedroom, my man cave, my office, my...well, you get the idea.) We are bombarded by more diversions than we can count. And thanks to companies from Atari to Apple, we have a vast variety of options to cultivate and enable couch potatoes far and wide. (Sadly, many of us getting wider and wider!)

In past generations many teenagers had to get jobs to help support the family, or at least earn their own spending or college money. Now great numbers of young people make it all the way to eighteen—some of them beyond if they go to college for four years without gainful employment—never having filled out a W4 form or even having so much as a babysitting job or doing manual labor of any kind!

Parents (especially mommas) don't want little Johnny or Suzie to have to over exert themselves. Mom and Dad want the fruit of their loins to enjoy the time of adolescence. (Adolescence: a concept only used by Western cultures. When I was growing up adolescence ran from 13 to 18. Today, pin-headed physiologists claim adolescence now lasts till 32.) Consequently, parents allow their young adults to hang out at home, attached to some sort of electronic device with their behinds firmly planted on a couch or chair cushion, "protected" from having to do much of anything.

Too many kids don't even have the responsibility to do chores of any sort around the house, and in the end we are creating citizens who simply have no work ethic. We are raising up generations of Lazy Asses. Young men and women who should be getting serious about life and their contribution to our communities, churches, and country, are instead going to college or technical school on their parents' dime--not because they want to get an education and be a contributing member of society or get married and start a family, but because they don't want to get a real job! They hang out at the folks' house, eating the folks' food, plugged into the folks' WIFI and sponge

DON'T BE AN ASS

off good old Mom and Pop.

And guess what? Lazy Ass kids frequently turn into Lazy Ass adults who continue to live lives wrapped in a blanket called "entitlement"; a Lazy Ass lifestyle perpetuated and promoted by everyone and everything around them – even the government. We are surrounded by people who won't get a decent job (or any job at all); people who won't marry (or even date) because they can't or won't commit to something or someone. The greatest commitment they can make involves a devotion to the TV screen long enough to binge watch five seasons of *Breaking Bad*. Then they and whine and complain on Facebook and Twitter or on blog posts that the country and the system is unfair because they don't have what someone else has. (By the way, the people who have all those things - those people actually got off their butts, worked, and did something for what they have achieved!)

What the Lazy Ass fails to recognize is that people who have great lives have them ON PURPOSE. A great life doesn't *just happen*. A great life doesn't exist *just because* you hope or wish for it. It's not because you're lucky or cute. People who are successful--those who have good jobs, thriving families and a flourishing faith--have those things because they were intentional about going after them.

They worked; they sacrificed; they put forth effort and committed themselves to a job well done.

A Lazy Ass exerts as little energy as possible and lacks production or progress for one amazing reason: He simply doesn't feel like it. He'll stay in bed until the last possible minute and then scramble to get out the door to arrive at a job a few minutes late, to do sub-par work at a job where he will never advance and then wonder why Fred in the next cubicle received a promotion with a pay increase and he did not. Mr. Lazy Ass will think it's because Fred is "just lucky", when, in fact, Fred *felt* like staying in bed, too. He could have used the extra thirty minutes to snooze, but instead, Fred got up and spent the time being intentional about his life. He also made sure he got to work *on time* and went the extra mile to dazzle the boss and go beyond what was expected of him…even though Fred may have *felt* like telling his boss where to stick it! You see, the thing about people who do life on purpose is…*they do not follow their feelings!*

> People who have great lives have them ON PURPOSE.

Our culture has bought into the lie that you don't have to do things if you don't feel like it. Parenting experts write books and our schools teach this nonsense: "Okay, Billy, you let me know when you feel like picking up the mess you made. Until then, you can choose to do something else." It's all about choice and not forcing kids to do what they don't *feel* like doing. (Can't damage their self-esteem, I guess.) How about teaching our kids that sometimes you just have to do the right thing, regardless of how you *feel*?

Many spouses—especially husbands, but wives, too—may *feel* like tossing their commitments to fidelity and to their marriage. Let's face it, being married is hard work—work that is worth it and has a tremendous payoff if you stick with it—but it is not always easy. You may not *feel* like investing in your marriage by spending time with your wife. You may not *feel* like giving your hubby that roll in the hay he's been hinting at. The Lazy Ass won't do those things. He'll opt to stay glued to his iPhone; she'll refuse to miss that episode of *The Bachelor*. And when their relationship stinks, when their marriage fails and their life sucks, they'll wonder WHY?

It doesn't take an astrophysicist with six advanced degrees to figure this out, people! Reaping and sowing. You get what you put into it.

Oh...and by the way...the ULTIMATE in Lazy Assedness is men

who waste their time and sexual energy on porn and masturbation. (And sometimes it's women with the "mommy porn" books.) It's the epitome of lazy! A man or woman who won't give his or her time and energy to be a lover to their spouse because "it's just easier to watch the screen or read the book and take care of myself" is pitiful. Nothing screams LAZY louder than that.

Don't be a Lazy Ass or a Half Ass. Get some discipline for goodness sake! Start small and set manageable goals. Take your spouse out on a date night once or twice a month. Spend time with your kids this week. Get to work early or *on time* for a change. (Or for some people, FIND a job!) Turn off the TV, put down your phone. Better for you to voluntarily get some self-discipline, than for life to force it on you.

> Reaping and sowing. You get what you put into it.

"Lazy hands make for poverty, but diligent hands bring wealth."
–Proverbs 10:4

This can be applied to financial income, but it could also lead to poverty in your relationships because you didn't exert yourself or invest in your spouse and children. It could be poverty in

DON'T BE AN ASS

your spirit simply because you didn't tend to the matters of your faith: prayer, church attendance, volunteering. King Solomon once wrote,

"Through laziness, the rafters sag; because of idle hands, the house leaks." – Ecclesiastes 10:18

Is your house sagging? How about your career? Your family? Your spiritual life? Your marriage?

"But I do go to church…twice a year…whether I need it or not."

"I did take my wife on a date…six months ago."

"I do make love to my husband…every six to eight weeks."

"I work hard at my job…when the boss is looking."

Discipline yourself to leave Lazy Ass and Half Ass behind. Commit (for real) to being the best version of yourself that you can be for those who love and depend on you.

> Our culture has bought the lie that you don't have to do things if you don't feel like it.

DON'T BE AN ASS

CHAPTER 3: Don't Be a Hard Ass

Someone who is a tough guy/chick; an arrogant blow-hard.

~ 19 ~

> A close cousin to the Jack Ass, the Hard Ass can be easily distinguished by his propensity to act and talk tough, and by his unrelenting and oh-so-arrogant demeanor.

He flaunts an awful lot of huff and puff that postures him as Mr. Hard Ass. He knows how things are supposed to be and there is no margin for deviation. There's a female version of the Hard Ass – she may earn the derogatory description of wench, witch or another word that rhymes with witch.

Hard Asses are "wannabes" who feel the need to prove how much they know, how much they can handle, and who they can take on. They act way too hardcore and intrusive for their own good. He will take on the bank teller for serving someone before him in another drive-up lane. She will rebuke the bag boy at the grocery store for giving her paper instead of plastic. He will give an ear full to the pastor in the lobby on a Sunday morning because he disagreed with an illustration used in the sermon. Ever combative, they are uncompromising and unrelenting in their opinions.

DON'T BE AN ASS

> "Hard Asses are "wannabes" who feel the need to prove how much they know, how much they can handle, and who they can take on."

And one of their favorite places to bluster, correct and exercise a lack of mercy and heavy hand of judgment? The Internet. The Internet is a giant magnet for the Hard Ass. It's like a pig rolling in slop-heaven! What a great place to view Hard Asses in action! Just browse the posts on Facebook, skim through the Tweets, spend time perusing the comments on a blog post or article. (You'll probably wish you hadn't.) It's the perfect venue for a Hard Ass to troll and to manifest his or her arrogance and malevolence toward mankind. And why not? It's cloaked in the safety of anonymity where unbridled braggadocio and swagger are freely expressed.

Generally speaking, one who falls into the Hard Ass category behaves as if his sense of humor has been surgically removed. Mr. Hard Ass is always quite serious and has no room for any level of joking or merriment. Exaggeration and hyperbole escape his mental capacity due to the fact that he is such a literal thinker. He holds you to "exactly what you said!!" Inflexible. Unbending. Intolerant. Always right. In short: A Hard Ass.

The Hard Ass is the nitpicker of life. If every jot and tittle isn't precisely right, they will take issue with it. "You said to meet you at the movie theater at 4:45! It was almost 4:50 before you got here! I was just about ready to leave because I didn't think you were going to show up!" Oy! Hard Asses' standards and protocols are fashioned out of steel—unbending and unyielding. They are stubborn people and show no hint of flexibility in their thinking. And when it comes to offering any morsel of forgiveness...forget about it! Offend the Hard Ass, and you'd better be prepared for the fallout.

A prime example of this is told in the "Parable of the Unmerciful Servant" recorded in Matthew 18:

[23] *"Therefore, the kingdom of heaven is like a king who wanted to settle accounts with his servants.*

[24] *As he began the settlement, a man who owed him ten thousand bags of gold was brought to him.*

[25] *Since he was not able to pay, the master ordered that he and his wife and his children and all that he had be sold to repay the debt.*

[26] *"At this the servant fell on his knees before him. 'Be patient*

with me,' he begged, 'and I will pay back everything.'

²⁷ *The servant's master took pity on him, canceled the debt and let him go.*

²⁸ *"But when that servant went out, he found one of his fellow servants who owed him a hundred silver coins. He grabbed him and began to choke him. 'Pay back what you owe me!' he demanded.*

²⁹ *"His fellow servant fell to his knees and begged him, 'Be patient with me, and I will pay it back.'*

³⁰ *"But he refused. Instead, he went off and had the man thrown into prison until he could pay the debt.*

Wow – the ultimate Hard Ass.

The servant showed no mercy to his fellow man; he exhibited no leniency, and cut him absolutely no slack! Did it matter one iota to him that he, himself, was forgiven of *way* more? Nope. Did he consider the *huge* debt of his own that he, undoubtedly, had no way or no hope of ever repaying? No, siree, Bob! In the world of the Hard Ass, there is no room for grace. No charity. No clemency for the offender.

The Hard Ass comes across as very tough, very thick-skinned. But don't be fooled! This tough, hard, shell-like exterior is only a front for fear and insecurity. He may bellow and blow a lot of steam, but

> "In the world of the Hard Ass, there is no room for grace."

it is only smoke and mirrors designed to hide what is really going on inside. He bobs and weaves, fists cocked in a show of toughness ala "You-want-a-piece-of me!?" on the outside, while on the inside, he's anything but.

His facade says, "I don't need you. I don't want you." Below the thin surface layer he wonders, "Why would you want me anyway? I'll never be good enough." So he keeps it all in check and disguises his lack of confidence and uncertainty with a rigid veneer.

If this is you, take a step back, get a grip and realize that no one survives as a lone wolf on the prairie. We need others. Life isn't a game of "Survivor" where the biggest Hard Ass, the most arrogant cutthroat left alone on the island at the end wins. Living with others isn't easy. Yes, they will cross you, hurt you, let you down, and make you mad. And, no, you just can't cast them all off your island. You have to forgive and you must learn to be proficient in dispensing mercy.

DON'T BE AN ASS

"Do not judge, and you will not be judged. Do not condemn and you will not be condemned. Forgive, and you will be forgiven."
- Luke 6:37

Whatever it is you think someone has done to you, whatever you think you are justified in hanging on to, whatever hurt you refuse to let go, whatever you can tally up as trespasses against you...none of it gets you a free ride on the train of UNforgiveness. Believe me, you will pay dearly to ride this train. Let it go. Learn to forgive and as The Golden Rule says, *"Do unto others as you would have them do unto you."*

> You have to forgive and you must learn to be proficient in dispensing mercy.

You might say, "Yeah, but Pastor! You don't know what they did to me!" Stop being such a Hard Ass and get it through your hard head that nothing is beyond mercy. Think about what *you* have been forgiven...even when you didn't deserve it...and cut your spouse, your friends, your parents, your pastor and everyone else some slack.

CHAPTER 4:
Don't Be a Dumb Ass

A person who continually does stupid things. Someone with no forward radar or ability to use logic or comprehend consequences.

**Let's face it—
anyone can make mistakes. Anyone.**

Every human being has a list of things they wish they *hadn't* done, or *had* done, or had done *differently*. For some of us, the list is painfully long; for others it's pretty short. But just because we've erred along the way and stumbled and bumbled over some of the choices of life, it doesn't automatically put us *all* into the Dumb Ass category.

Obviously, at any given time, one can give rise to what would be titled a "dumbass" decision, mistake, or mishap. A choice made where the repercussions and consequences were not clearly thought through. Most of the time, one learns from the pain of those lessons and opts to act differently in the future so as to not repeat the series of unfortunate events again. What makes a person a member of the Dumb Ass club is when one continuously lacks any sense of forward

DON'T BE AN ASS

radar and consistently operates under a shortfall of common sense or logic. A Dumb Ass not only lives in an apparent vacuum, void of an ability to consider the consequences of his or her actions, he or she perpetually and stubbornly refuse to stop the stupid even when someone points out the asininity of their behaviors.

A married woman who—without thinking it through—goes to lunch alone with a male co-worker and then realizes he has more in mind than just grabbing a quick bite at McDonalds and would rather grab something else, has put herself into a precarious position. That was probably a dumbass decision. But if she recognizes the fact that, "Uh oh! This was a bad idea!" and doesn't feed into the conversation with the man, quickly as possible ends the lunchtime encounter, then does not accept invitations from opposite-sex friends or acquaintances again, she is *not* what we would term a Dumb Ass.

On the other hand...a married woman who continually attends lunches with a man—alone— even after her husband has objected and communicated that he is uncomfortable with such an arrangement; a woman who defends her actions by saying, "But we're only friends!"... *she* is a certifiable Dumb Ass. Such behavior leads to the most perilous of ends.

The man who continues to repeat a behavior that annoys his wife, even though she has made it expressly clear that she does not like when he engages in the behavior, and it leads to arguments every time… is a Dumb Ass. For example: Acting in rude and insulting ways every time her mother comes over by cracking crude jokes or making belittling or disrespectful remarks. The man who persists with this is intentionally causing trouble in his marriage — not to mention running the risk of sleeping on the couch for an indefinite amount of time.

Unfortunately, talking to the Dumb Ass is like talking to a wall. Good advice or solemn warning bounces off like raindrops on a newly waxed car.

Listen to advice and accept discipline, and at the end you will be counted among the wise. – Proverbs 19:20

> A Dumb Ass stubbornly refuses to stop the stupid even when someone points out the asininity of the behavior.

DON'T BE AN ASS

The Dumb Asses of the world, unless they change their ways, will most definitely *not* be counted among the wise. Despite the best efforts of those around him to cast light on the faultiness and foolishness of his thinking and behavior patterns, a Dumb Ass will continue his shortsighted habits. Common sense should tell a person that doing the same thing with the same result is just stupid. But, as the saying goes, common sense isn't as common as one would think.

Dealing with a Dumb Ass on the job can be extraordinarily taxing. One looks in wonder upon this person and thinks, "Exactly *how* did you get this job?" He seems to have no sense of urgency; no ability to see that what he does or doesn't do in his role has direct implications for other co-workers. He has no idea how he cripples their ability to complete tasks, to perform on projects, and to fulfill their duties. The Dumb Ass frequently walks around as if in some sort of invisible bubble, totally unaware that his conduct has any bearing on the rest of the world. Clueless.

Sometimes Dumb Assery is not about doing the *same* stupid thing repeatedly, but rather, it's making one colossally dumbass decision after another. Decisions one knows will not go over well in the marital relationship. Things like: buying a boat without consulting your wife; going rogue and purchasing a new car after having a discussion with your husband where he clearly said that it's best for your budget to wait another year; opening an account to secretly stash money so your spouse doesn't know and can't get access to it; changing the passwords for your computer, phone, or lock screen on your cable when the two of you have agreed to always share such information.

Do you see the common thread in these kinds of actions? Selfishness. It's all about what *I* want and how *I* want things to be. I have news for you… LIFE ISN'T JUST ABOUT YOU! It's not about what *you* want all the time. All relationships—and especially marriage—need to be more about the "us" and the "we" than the "me, me, me, me!" Pay attention to other people around you. Think it through: How will my actions impact another? If I do A, what will happen? What will the ramifications be? If I do B, instead, will I get better/different results?

A large part of the Dumb Ass problem is that impetuousness and instant gratification have become the faulty foundation upon which people build their lives. No one wants to wait for anything. We live in a culture of microwave minutes, overnight shipping, and instant downloads. Why on earth would a person have to wait for anything?

DON'T BE AN ASS

More importantly, why *should* they? Isn't life all about being happy? Getting what I want? Having things *my way*? No, in fact, it's not.

Self-help gurus who tout the key to happiness is taking care of yourself and looking out for number one, and TV preachers who preach the mantra: *God wants you to be happy*, are doing us a grave disservice. The live in-the-moment, fly-by-the-seat-of-your-pants, follow-your-feelings, damn-the-consequences kind of thinking just doesn't lead to good results. If it is what you are grounding your life's decisions on, you are most assuredly not going to like the outcomes.

> All relationships—and especially marriage—need to be about the "us" and the "we", not the "me, me, me, me!"

And, of particular note when it comes to the making of a straight-up Dumb Ass, is the special kind of stupid that comes from making decisions on the basis of sex and lust. (This goes for both women and men!) Despite the excitement that deludes you into thinking your wildest dreams and deepest needs will be met through this other person, the sexual tryst usually ends up with relatives who despise you, friends who are embarrassed by you, children who are wounded by you, and a spouse who is devastated by you. The sheer number of people who are negatively impacted by a Dumb Ass sexual encounter is stunning.

Want to check out a couple of very sordid tales of guys who were quintessential Dumb Asses motivated and driven by sexual desire? Read the accounts of Sampson and David in the Old Testament. Both men encountered a spiral of tragedy that is breathtaking. Although both came to see the error of their ways and achieved some level of redemption, make no mistake, each suffered grave consequences due to choices they made that were inspired by their loins rather than their brains. A healthy dose of forward radar could have saved them both—and those around them— a boatload of grief.

Just like the Lazy Ass, the Dumb Ass has no concept of reaping and sowing. He simply does not have the forethought or moral aptitude to do the math on most things and figure out there is a little principle called "cause and effect" in life. For the Dumb Ass, it seems beyond reason to imagine that humans could actually use solid judgment or rational thought in the decisions they make. People who act rashly with little prudence or planning, or those who lack discretion and just live by impulse and emotion, do so at great threat to their present and future life. (Not to mention the lives of those around them.) So what is the remedy for those who are stuck on the lack-of-logic merry-go-round and can't seem to step off?

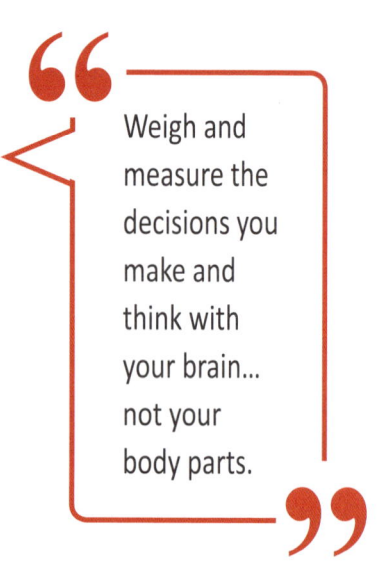

> "Weigh and measure the decisions you make and think with your brain... not your body parts."

    Get counsel. Seek wisdom. Listen to advice.

    Despite the obvious positive implications of asking for advice from others before acting, many people plow forward all the time making foolish decisions based on faulty premises and give no thought to what will happen down the road. Will the choices you make today fall apart and unravel in the future? Will they yield the best possible outcomes? Will they have a negative impact on or hurt others?

    Don't be a Dumb Ass. Consider the consequences—both good and bad. Weigh and measure the decisions you make and think with your brain...not your body parts. Get wise counsel and advice from people who know you; people who are familiar with your situation, and can speak into your life from an intelligent perspective.

> *"...the prudent give thought to their steps."* - Proverbs 14:14

Remember, Dumb Ass, it's not just you who suffers the consequences of your behavior. Don't let the path you walk become littered with wounded family members, peers, and friends simply because you failed to take time to give careful thought to your actions.

DON'T BE AN ASS

CHAPTER 5:
Don't Be a Smart Ass

Someone who is wise in his own eyes and always has a smart-aleck answer for everything. One who takes nothing seriously and makes no productive contributions.

~ 37 ~

Nobody likes a Smart Ass— or so the saying goes.

Actually, the Smart Asses of the world can make a great first impression, and tend to be quite charming, funny and charismatic. They have a refined sense of humor that most people find quite engaging and initially the hilarious interplay is enjoyable – lots of laughter and smiles. The allure of such a personality can be hypnotizing and the Smart Ass will suck you in…and then pull you under. What was once enchanting and entertaining now becomes a relentless string of annoying, aggravating and often cruel punch lines.

While bringing a great degree of levity to an oh-too-serious world, the non-stop volley of inane commentary can be outright frustrating when one is trying to conduct business, resolve conflict or deal with the more deliberate things of life. Try discussing finances with a spouse who won't answer a direct question or contribute

DON'T BE AN ASS

anything to the conversation but one-liners and inane quips. Asking a Smart Ass mate for suggestions on how to deal with the discipline of your children will produce all kinds of fodder for a Jimmy Fallon monologue, yet profit nothing in terms of useful input.

One of the most trying aspects of talking to a Smart Ass is you most frequently have no idea if he or she is joking or serious. Was there some truth to that retort? Was it sarcasm or some thinly veiled insult? Even when it is covered by insisting, "I was just joking!" it leaves those on the receiving end of the acerbic wit a bit dazed and confused.

Like a maniac shooting flaming arrows of death
is one who deceives their neighbor and says, "I was only joking!"
– Proverbs 26:18 & 19

Maniac? Flaming arrows of death? Sounds pretty serious, but you Smart Asses reading that passage will probably just find a way to make another joke! You'd even tell Solomon to "lighten up!"

Always the devoted jokesters, Smart Asses will horse around, act like a clown, jab, gibe or rib those around them ad nauseam, and think it's extraordinarily amusing and funny. They will quip, mock and wisecrack about the most austere subjects. And because they tend to be self-deprecating, nothing is off limits: your job, family, parenting skills, physical appearance, your mistakes and insecurities – it's all fair game. You may try to explain to them that it's only funny if the other person thinks it's funny, but those words have very little impact on the Smart Ass. They won't understand and typically care very little how their words hurt you or others. In some cases, it just adds fuel to the fire. When they know they can goad you and get under your skin, hard-core Smart Asses will gorge on the banquet of your discomfort. They may not even see it as cruel or think that their humor is at your expense; to them, it's just amusing.

Don't be cruel...especially in front of others. It's one thing if you and your spouse, your kids, your friends, family, or co-workers can share in playful and fun-loving banter. Lots of us have that kind of relationship with people...sort of like the Frank and Marie Barone dynamic from the TV series *Everybody Loves Raymond.* Actually, the whole family is quite versed in the art of the one liner. But when the good-natured kidding that is okay in private becomes slicing and dicing

> One of the most trying aspects of talking to a Smart Ass is you frequently have no idea if he is joking or serious.

in public, it crosses over the line and is anything but enjoyable.

Learning to give it back is one of the best ways to combat the Smart Ass, but this tactic comes with a word of caution: Many people of this ilk can dish it out…but they can't take it. The exact words she uses toward you may in turn wound and offend the Smart Ass when applied to her. He may not find it nearly as droll when the zingers start hitting him below the belt. It's one of the characteristics that makes a Smart Ass so exasperating.

Understand that a Smart Ass isn't always a Smart Ass. Sometimes he can be quite serious. It may only be 1% of the time, but he does, indeed, have sober and earnest moments. And woe to those who don't actually pick up on that rare occasion! The poor, indignant Smart Ass then complains that others don't take him seriously! Really!?

"Whoever keeps his mouth and tongue keeps himself out of trouble." – Proverbs 21:23 ESV

Many a Smart Ass has found herself in difficulties and disagreements and yet remains completely clueless as to how such troubles occurred. Little does she realize that it was the lack of guard over her mouth or restraint on her spicy comebacks that led to the demise in the first place.

"Whoever belittles his neighbor lacks sense" - Proverbs 11:12

In contrast to this warning in Proverbs, we've heard studies that say people with a penchant for sarcasm and quick wit are more intelligent. (Wait...maybe that was just a meme I saw on Facebook.) Clearly Smart Asses think themselves to be quite brilliant and astute. But while the label is "Smart" Ass, unless there is a degree of caution or self-control, one can quickly end up in the "Dumb" Ass category. (See the previous chapter.)

"Death and life are in the power of the tongue, and those who love it will eat its fruits." - Proverbs 18:21

DEATH? Most people are unaware of the power wielded by their words. I've had a great number of men and women in my office lamenting the pain caused by something mean or careless that their parents, a spouse, a boss, a friend, or sibling said...sometimes decades ago. Of course, we need to work on letting go and forgiving them, but make no mistake, there is great potential to wound others with our

DON'T BE AN ASS

smart aleck comments and wisenheimer cracks. Despite the children's rhyme about sticks and stones, apparently words *can* hurt.

> Most people are unaware of the power wielded by their words.

And let's face it—sometimes we just want to be taken seriously! There is little that shouts, "I don't really take you, our relationship or your troubles seriously!!" louder than a steady discourse of wise-assery.

In the normal course of life, all of us say things we wish we could take back. Think of it like toothpaste squeezed out of the tube... you can't put it back in. Such is the problem with words: Once they are spoken, the mess is made. Try as you may, they won't go back in. The best you can do is to clean up the mess you created as a result of your careless words, but sometimes that is much easier said than done.

It can be outright discouraging to those on the receiving end when what could and should be a genuine statement of encouragement is wrapped in a veneer of sarcasm or outright slams... all in "good fun." (At least according to the Smart Ass delivering them.) Hey, wise guy! Just because you think it's amusing, the rest of the world around you may not be so entertained.

Listen up, Smart Ass. You are not always as funny as you think you are. Learn to curb the incessant need to make everything a joke. The irksome smart-aleck comebacks really do wear thin. People don't know where they stand with you. They don't know whether you said what you meant or meant what you said. At the end of the day, they don't ever really get to know you...what you really think or feel... because you are so quick to brandish your protective shield of buffoonery.

I am not saying you cannot be your witty and entertaining self. I'm just pleading: Give your wife, your kids, your friends and all the people you work with a break. Dummy up and put a muzzle on it...at least some of the time. Really, those around you would like it if you would ease up on the shenanigans. They might come to see you and know you as someone other than the eternal clown. By toning down the remarks and comebacks and daring to sprinkle some sincerity into your communication, you may actually confer a sense of caring and consideration to people and become a contributing member of your family and place of employment. Because at the end of the day...no one really likes a constant Smart Ass.

CHAPTER 6:
Don't Be a Bad Ass

Someone who is an ego driven user. A narcissist who lives according to his or her own rules.

> **When one's sense of self-importance is over inflated, and the ego is out of control, he or she has a tendency to be what we would term a Bad Ass.**

Rather than exercising humility, Bad Asses are enamored with their own self-worth and are ruthless in their pursuit of selfish gain.

When the ego is in the driver's seat, be assured that the destination will only be a dead end when it comes to relationships. Oh, a Bad Ass can come off as in command, self-confident, even cool and hip. I am often amazed by the number of women who are drawn to a Bad Ass—he can ooze such charm and charisma. But in the end these women are like moths drawn to the candle's flame—bursting in agonizing pain as they are consumed and destroyed by the very thing that seem so alluring.

Don't be fooled. At the end of the day, Bad Asses have a singular goal: to fulfill their own conceit and vanity. They truly have no regard for others outside of using them as a means to their own narcissistic end. And once you have satisfied his selfish needs, once he has used you to achieve his purpose, the Bad Ass will find some other unwitting soul to prey upon for his self-gratification.

Yet, despite all the warning signs, many a poor body is duped into thinking a Bad Ass is quite a gem of a person, simply because the allure and appeal can be quite bewitching. Mr. Smooth is quite clever at camouflaging his egocentric ways until he's wrung every drop out of his prey.

No Bad Ass will come right out and say, *"Let me use you to the utmost degree for my own intents and purposes."* Au contraire...they will flatter and sweet talk others giving the impression that they are genuine in their praise, when all the while *"they flatter others for their own advantage."* – Jude 1:16

A Bad Ass will exploit those around him for anything from financial increase and career advancement to sexual gain for no other reason except life is all about him. He lives in the center of his own universe and he has an insatiable need to feed his ego.

There are no guidelines or regulations on behavior for a Bad Ass. Rules don't apply—at least not the standard social or ethical rules that govern healthy people. The only regulations he lives by are his own. After all, who could possibly qualify to dictate the direction of his life? A Bad Ass has no regard for authority because he is the authority. So convinced, is he, of his own maxed-out ultra-coolness, there is no need to descend to the level of dealing with the constraints that govern the less-than-bad-ass others of the world.

The sign says NO PARKING? Forget that! She'll park her shiny Cadillac there if she wants to. He can flirt (or worse) with women other than his wife. The line is too long so she cuts in front. All the policies and procedures of the office are meaningless to him. The Bad Asses of the world are those who don't keep appointments, show up late with no apology, repeatedly break promises, and fail to fulfill their obligations. They take no responsibility nor do they show any remorse, but rather blame the other person: "It's your fault I forgot. You didn't remind me."

Along with no respect for rules, they also have no need of sincere feeling and consider any such display of fear or emotions a weakness. She will never allow herself a vulnerable moment. He will never tolerate emotional display from another person. Trying to have a meaningful conversation or showing transparency will most likely never happen in a relationship. Bad Asses are self-absorbed and have

DON'T BE AN ASS

little empathy or concern about the feelings of others. They love to talk about themselves and won't give others much of a chance to participate in a two-way conversation. All chatter tends to be about them. He will interrupt quickly and switch the focus back to himself. She will show little genuine interest in you as you struggle to have your point of view heard. When you do manage to get a word in, if she doesn't agree with you, your ideas will most likely be corrected or discarded altogether. Emotions and genuine connection are foreigners in the land of Bad Ass. Unless, of course, used to advance their agenda and reach their objective.

> A Bad Ass has no regard for authority because he is the authority.

Bad Asses have a no-holds-barred attitude and will bully, cheat and lie to achieve the goals of their egomaniacal life. He thinks nothing of taking credit for something you did at work. She will throw you under the bus in front of another person just to make herself look good. It borders on the ridiculous to watch the lengths a Bad Ass will go to in order to put others down. Mr. Full-of-Himself is oh-so-skilled in the ability to fluff up his delusions of grandeur. The fish stories that a Bad

Ass can tell! He is never at a loss for hyperbole or exaggeration when dazzling others with tales of his greatness.

Imagine what life is like married to such a person. The incessant pompousness, the tedium at everything revolving around their universe, and ever knowing that when your spouse is extolling kindness to you, it is only to serve their own ego and desires. That beautiful diamond necklace he gave you for your anniversary was more about posting it on Facebook to look like "Man of the Year" and getting the strokes from the "likes" and comments. The way she gets all dolled up and decked out for that dinner party has less to do with looking nice for you and more to do with turning the heads and garnering attention from the other men in your social circle. Ahhhh... yes. Such is life with the ego-driven.

The Bad Ass is a user who can manipulate, mold and maneuver; often toying with the emotions of others just to get what he or she desires. In the dating world, there's a name for this guy (although, women can sometimes be guilty as well) - a player. A man or woman who, with good looks and charm, befriends you and makes you feel important before they use you for their own gain. And players make terrible spouses. Don't think for one second that a ring on that third-finger, left hand is some magic talisman that will cause him or her to trade in their player's card. During the dating process he may go to great lengths to convince you that you have "tamed him." She will give you all the right lines about how you're "the one" she was waiting for. Take my advice and RUN!!

Bad Asses believe the world revolves around them. Others are supposed to cater to their needs, whims and wishes. Life operates entirely on their agenda. Because of their narcissism, Bad Asses are one of the most trying types of Asses to deal with. Lack of humility makes it difficult for them to see their flaws.

Do nothing out of selfish ambition or vain conceit. Rather, in humility value others above yourselves, not looking to your own interests, but each of you to the interests of others. —Philippians 2:4

People don't like to be used. They don't like to be treated as a commodity. There is a saying that goes like this: "People were created to be loved and things were created to be used." Sadly, the world is in chaos today because things are being loved, and people are being used.

If this Bad Ass description applies to you, and you want to change, here are some suggestions: Try to become self-aware. (As opposed to just self-ish.) Step back a bit. Look at what you are doing. Be intentional. Dropping the self-centered, egotistical behavior will go a long way in curbing the chaos in your marriage, family and other relationships.

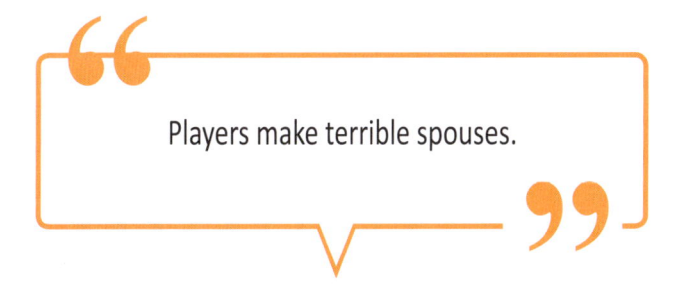

> Players make terrible spouses.

CHAPTER 7:

Don't Be a Cheap Ass

Someone who is stingy with time, money, emotion, and love.

> **Let's face it, how one spends money says a lot about what kind of person they are.**

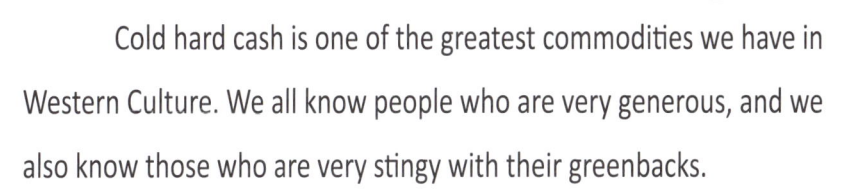

Cold hard cash is one of the greatest commodities we have in Western Culture. We all know people who are very generous, and we also know those who are very stingy with their greenbacks.

Now, don't think that everyone who is thrifty with his or her money is automatically a Cheap Ass. There are people who pride themselves on being frugal. They are bargain shoppers who find the best deals and squeeze the most out of every dollar they have. And even in their thriftiness, they can be quite generous. On the other hand, there are people who—regardless of how much money they have—are so tight that they squeak when they walk.

Some folks intentionally live small just so they can *give* large, while others give small so they can *live* large. It's a choice. Studies have shown that those who are the most generous givers are not the very

DON'T BE AN ASS

wealthy. One such study conducted by the *Chronicle of Philanthropy* found that households earning $50,000 to $75,000 give an average of 7.6 percent of their discretionary income to charity, compared with an average of 4.2 percent for people who make $100,000 or more. You see, our propensity to give isn't about the size of our bank accounts… it's about the size of our hearts.

Oftentimes, the least-financially endowed, yet wise-spenders are also the most generous, while some of the richest people can be the biggest Cheap Asses when it comes to generosity toward others. No, Cheap Asses are not defined merely by the amount of money they have and spend. Cheap Asses are defined by their level of selfishness… the overwhelming trait of any Ass. Cheap Asses simply do not want to share. The refrain they sing is like that of the seagulls in the movie *Finding Nemo*: MINE! MINE! MINE! They whine and bellyache that they have no money and couldn't possibly help others because they are so broke. Yet, surprisingly they always seem to find the money to spend on what *they* want to buy. And as you can imagine, a Cheap Ass spouse can be quite difficult to live with for that very reason.

He will find money in the budget for the purchases that he wants to make, yet cry, "We're broke! Don't spend any more money!"

when it comes to things that are important to the wife or the rest of the family. Funny how spending isn't an issue when the Cheap Ass drives through Starbucks or whips out the credit card at Costco for things that are absolute "necessities" for him! The problem isn't the money that *he* spends; the problem is always the money that his spouse spends. Again, Cheap Asses don't like to share.

And it isn't just about money. So it is with other important commodities such as time, emotions, and affections. Cheap Asses don't want to give anything to anyone. They are the tightwads of time, paupers of affection, and guardians to the vault of emotion. These are the people who just cannot conceive of loving any child other than the ones that come from their own loins (even if they marry and create a blended family). "No, no, no! I could not *possibly* show concern or tenderness to any other child." (As if affection had limits like a checkbook!)

You see the Cheap Ass only sees lack. The glass is always half empty. There just isn't enough of anything to go around. Everything in life is a commodity to be horded – like the survivalist that fills his basement with toilet paper. If a neighbor asks for a spare roll they would be rebuffed. "I haven't got a square to spare!" (A special nod to all the *Seinfeld* fans.) "No, no, no, I must guard every precious roll. There might not be enough!" After all, when the zombie apocalypse hits the most important thing will not be to keep your brains from being eaten by hungry zombies – it will be all about maintaining the proper hygiene after pooping!

The Cheap Ass is too busy to spend time with their spouse, their kids, their parents, their friends; always having somewhere else to go or something more important to do. To be sure, some people truly are busy. They give of themselves to their job, their kids, grandkids, friends, family, church and the list can go on and on. Don't assume that because someone doesn't have time right now for you, that he is being selfish and a Cheap Ass with his time. More often than not, these are the people that give extraordinary amounts of time to love and serve and give to others. True Cheap Asses make excuses or seem like they are so busy with all the demands of life—when the reality is they just want to sit at home and watch another Netflix marathon, play another round of golf or indulge in non-stop video games for the weekend. A Cheap Ass can't possibly set aside any time for those in his circle because everything is about him. Just like his money, he also hoards his time.

On the outside chance that you actually get her to commit to that volunteer project or get him to compromise and spend time with family, be forewarned -- they will most likely make it clear how much of their valuable time you have wasted; how this was such a huge sacrifice and how you are now indebted to them because sixty minutes of their precious time was so lavishly offered up and then frivolously used by you. *SIGH*

> Our propensity to give isn't about the size of our bank accounts...it's about the size of our hearts.

It's why so many who live with a Cheap Ass don't bother to ask for anything. The residual moaning and lament aren't worth the trade off and are enough to try the patience of anyone.

Granted, we all need our "alone" time, our hanging out with the boys' day, or our girls' night out. It is wise to relax, chill and have fun and exercise care with the margins in our life. There are appropriate boundaries for our time, just like there are appropriate limits with our money when it comes to spending and giving. No one is suggesting that *all* of our time and *all* of our money have to be given away. But the Cheap Ass gives next to no time and practically no money to others. All of it is spent exclusively on his or her self-centered desires.

Being a Scrooge with one's time is especially problematic in a marriage and family. And generally speaking, this is typically more of a man thing, but some women are guilty, too. So if the shoe fits, madam... A guy who works 40, 50, 60 plus hours a week, then fills up the remainder of his waking hours with hobbies such as hunting, fishing, sports, or video games, never giving any of his time or attention to his wife and children is only selfish and a big old Cheap Ass with his time. Same goes for a working woman who spends all of her extra time consistently shopping at the mall, hanging out with girlfriends, working out at the gym, or lost for hours on Pinterest or Facebook, never affording any attention to her husband or family. Not only are they selfish but they are also risking their marriages and families by never being around or never engaging with their loved ones.

It takes intention to make a great marriage. You raise great kids on purpose. Couples have terrific sex lives because they are willful in their actions and make the time for each other. Not only do we have to give of our time to others, we also have to give of our emotion. It does no good to "just show up" without actually being present and contributing attention and affection. The Cheap Asses of the world are also misers of emotion, rationing compliments, kind words and affirmations like a World War II gas station attendant. They wouldn't dare want to give one hug too many or actually say the words, "I love you." After all –if they don't hold onto everything now, there might not be enough later.

    Cheap Asses think that by holding onto everything they actually give those things greater value, but nothing could be further from the truth. We actually show those around us that we value them when we *give* of our most precious commodities…our money, our time and ourselves. You want to have a great marriage, good friendships, strong bonds with your kids? Loosen the purse strings, the time clock and the muzzle. Be generous with your money, your time and your words and affection. Scriptures speak of the benefits of generosity…. for both the giver and receiver!

    A generous person will prosper; whoever refreshes others will be refreshed. - Proverbs 11:25

DON'T BE AN ASS

You want to prosper in your relationships? Heck, in life, period!? Let go of being cheap and tight with all you have to give. Want to be blessed? Learn to give. And remember what I said earlier about reaping and sowing in this life? Yep...it applies here, too. The Bible clearly teaches:

Whoever shows sparingly will also reap sparingly, and whoever sows generously will also reap generously. - 1 Corinthians 9:6

> We actually show those around us that we value them when we give of our most precious commodities... our money, our time and ourselves.

Ever hear the phrase, *you get what you give?* If you use a big old ten-gallon bucket when you pour into the lives of others, you will receive the same back. Man, sign me up for the bucket full of love and blessings! Amazingly, many Cheap Asses can't, for the life of themselves, figure out why they get such a scant amount back in life.

Give. Start today. Even if it's just a small token or a baby step.

(Remember Bill Murray in *What About Bob?*....baby steps!) Release the iron-fisted grip on your wallet. Spend ten bucks on something special for your spouse or your kids just to let them know you were thinking of them today. Devote a half hour of time and do something intentional to show you value them and that they are important to you. Give a kind word, a hug, or hold a hand. Dare to speak the words, "I love you." Sow the right seeds into your family that will grow into a rich harvest that all of you will benefit from.

CHAPTER 8:
Don't Be a Whiney Ass

Someone who is a constant whiner and complainer.

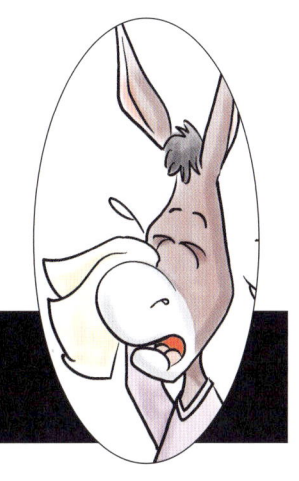

Ahhhhh…..the quintessential bellyacher! We all know them.

Perhaps it's a co-worker, a sister-in-law, or even one of your parents! Dealing with a Whiney Ass on a consistent basis is perplexing to say the least…but it is extraordinarily taxing to be married to this suck-the-life-out-of-you soul. Nothing. Is. Ever. Right.

Just going out to eat with Mr. or Ms. Whiner makes one long for starvation rather than being subjected to the griping and agonizing technicalities of a simple lunch at Applebee's. Pulling into the parking lot begins the unpleasant list of things that are wrong!

"Those people should not pull through the parking spaces. I never do that. Look at how that guy parked! He's too close to the car on the right. Park there!! It's easier to get out."

Really?? It presents *that* big of a challenge to watch your driver get the vehicle between two white lines on the blacktop?!

DON'T BE AN ASS

Choosing a table to sit at: Oh, wait! It has to be the RIGHT table! Not a table, a booth. Not that corner, the TV isn't at the right angle to see. No, the other side because the sun is shining in the windows on this side. Exasperated, the hostess *finally* arrives at a booth that seems to fit the endless list of criteria so King Fussbudget can plop his butt down. Then begins the arduous task of going through the menu! (See why one would wish it was a day of fasting!?)

"This isn't the same menu they had last time. Why do they change things so often? I just know I'm not going to find anything I like on this new menu. Wait...there is a shrimp special, but for heaven sake! Look how expensive it is! I'm not paying $13 for lunch." And then the poor server comes to the table...amidst loud whispers of, "It's about time!" (Apparently two minutes is a ridiculously long wait time.)

"Welcome to Applebee's! Can I start you off with something to drink?" says the smiley twenty-something gal...clearly, unaware of the fact that her smile will be greatly tested and tried by the man in the booth.

"I want iced tea. But not if it's that powdered crap. Only fresh brewed. Is it fresh brewed? Don't tell me it is if you are going to bring that awful instant stuff. But I want only three ice cubes in it. And a lemon slice, not a lemon wedge. Have you got that? You better write it down. Waitresses mess it up all the time. They can never get anything right."

Wow…just writing about this jacks up my blood pressure! As you can imagine, it doesn't get any better from here. The waitress brought the tea and, God forbid, there were four ice cubes and not three. He was certain that the tea was from powder and that the server lied. The thirteen specifications for his cheeseburger were also unmet, and of course, there was great debate over the amount of tip to leave the poor, frazzled girl…who really did her utmost to maintain that smile right up till the "Thank you for coming in! Have a nice day!" I'm sure her day was exceedingly better the moment Whiney Ass walked out the door. The Whiney Asses of the world are the nightmares of those in customer service jobs. That whole "the customer is always right" thing is truly put on trial when dealing with the chronic complainer.

They fuss, moan, whine, bellyache, complain about and take exception to nearly everything. All things in life are mountains, not molehills, and they literally go to war and choose to die on every one of those mountains as if the future of the free world depended upon whether the toaster was two inches to the left on the counter. How annoying is it that when you come home from the store and she doesn't praise you for remembering to buy the tissues, rather snivels, "I always buy the Puffs, not the Kleenex brand. And you should have gotten the blue box, not the yellow box because it matches the bathroom." Uugghh!

A drive through the neighborhood on a beautiful sunny summer day is anything but enjoyable when all one hears is a chorus of complaint:

"That guy shouldn't mow his lawn in a straight line; it should be mowed on a diagonal. Everyone knows that. What's the matter with that guy?

They should have put their trashcans away yesterday after the garbage man came. Why on earth would anyone leave their cans out another day?

Look at the way they have those flowers planted. That woman doesn't know anything about gardening.

Why did they build the deck off that side of their house? That's not the best design."

Sigh...for the love of heaven. Quit your bellyaching! Surely there has to be something that these unfettered narcissists find pleasing in the world! Nothing screams UNGRATEFUL like a person who rags and nags and carps about the sum total of all things in the existence of the planet. The incessant moaning about every ever-loving thing leads those around Captain Whiney-pants to want to scream, "Can't you just shut up and be grateful for *anything*?!"

It is extremely annoying to live life with a constant critic. The fault finder of all. I've got news for you Whiney Asses: It's not all about *you*! Just because the car ahead of you doesn't take off like a NASCAR driver when the light turns green, you shouldn't lay on the horn and act like the fates of the universe are conspiring against you to ruin your day! Your acting peevish and put out by those around you...by the way, it's *those* people who love you in spite of your continual griping, grousing and grumbling...is really, really exacting. You honestly think it's going to set your household into pandemonium if the heat is set at 71 and not 72 degrees?

> " Nothing screams UNGRATEFUL like a person who rags and nags and carps about the sum total of all things in the existence of the planet. "

DON'T BE AN ASS

Hey, Whiney Ass! Can you hear that constant sucking noise… it's the sound of the life and energy being drained from your spouse, kids, family and friends. For the love of God, STOP IT! The pettiness grows so old. The whining is enough to test the good graces of even Mother Teresa.

Moses had some pretty sobering words for the grumblers and whiners who accompanied him on The Exodus:

"You will know that it was the Lord when he gives you meat to eat in the evening and all the bread you want in the morning, because he has heard your grumbling against him. Who are we? You are not grumbling against us, but against the Lord." – Exodus 16:8

Did you catch that? When you grumble against all your circumstances in life, you are not grumbling against your neighbors, your kids, your spouse, your family or your coworkers; you are grumbling against God. Every time you open your yap and start yammering about all the things that are wrong, when you whine about this, that and the other, you are bemoaning what God himself has given you. That's what ingratitude does. That's what comes from an attitude of thanklessness.

"Don't grumble against one another, brothers and sisters, or you will be judged." – James 5:9

Apparently, even God gets sick of your whining. Start looking at what is good and right in your realm. Intentionally set out to develop some gratitude and thankfulness.

"Whatever is true, whatever is noble, whatever is right, whatever is pure, whatever is lovely, whatever is admirable—if anything is excellent or praiseworthy—think about such things."

– Philippians 4:8

I know, I know...some of you have a most difficult time seeing things as being lovely or admirable or excellent or praiseworthy. Change your filter and adjust the lens you are looking through. Start counting your blessings and end the niggling and nitpicking. We always, always, always have things to be grateful for in this life.

It is true, not everything is *exactly* the way we want it, but as the saying goes: *The happiest people don't have the best of everything, they just make the best of everything they have.* Believe me... your spouse, kids, family, friends and co-workers will be the *most* grateful.

> " We always, always, always have things to be grateful for in this life. "

DON'T BE AN ASS

CHAPTER 9:

Don't Be a Crazy Ass

Someone who overreacts and becomes emotionally unglued easily.

~ 71 ~

We all know at least one Crazy Ass person.

(Hopefully it's not the one you see in the mirror each morning!) It's the man or woman who has a hair-trigger reaction to *everything* in life and has a nuclear meltdown over the smallest of happenings. And while it is true that women tend to be more emotional than men, this is not about emotion - this is about crazy. And history, the nightly news and our own personal experiences with humanity prove that both men and women are equally as capable of coming unhinged.

Now, we all have our bad days, or moments when stress has fried and frazzled our very last nerve. You know, those instances when we answer our spouses with much too snappy of a tone, when our blood pressure and our voices get raised at the kids making too much noise in the living room or when the sigh and the eye roll slip out in front of that work colleague who asked the same stupid question for

DON'T BE AN ASS

the 67th time. Most people will admit that they've reacted badly at some point when just the right buttons get pushed and they sort of flip out. After all, we are only human and fatigue, impatience and annoyance can sometimes get the best of the best of us.

That doesn't land one as a member of Crazy Ass. Like all the other Asses, what earns a person membership is the repeated pattern of behaviors. We're talking about someone who consistently functions in a state of emotion disproportionate to the circumstance. You forgot to start the coffee maker when you got up this morning so your husband's java wasn't ready when he got out of the shower and the fireworks go off. She is absolutely distraught because a girlfriend invited someone else to go shopping and didn't include her. He reacts with unmitigated despair because someone else in the office got the promotion instead of him. You find yourself looking for the nearest fallout shelter after her bomb of fury explodes over the fact that the coach didn't play your kid in the fourth quarter of the game. Chronic and excessive emotional reaction is what defines a Crazy Ass. He or she has no capacity to deal with disappointment, frustration, upset or setbacks without unleashing the recoil of apocalyptic proportion.

Assuredly, there are some very difficult and tragic things in life that would elicit a more intense and emotive reaction, but to the Crazy Ass *everything* in life warrants such a response. Like the child who screams bloody murder, summoning all the adults in a three-block radius, only to discover that she sees a ladybug on the floor. The whole of life is a catastrophic event. It's quite exasperating and draining to those who have to live and work with such a person. It is also wearisome when friends, family and coworkers find it necessary to become "eggshell walkers" always looking out for their next step; constantly trying to avoid the land mines and second guessing and sidestepping what will set off the next round of emotional explosions. It's not so fun to be on the receiving end of all the drama and trauma of those who live in the perpetual state of crazy.

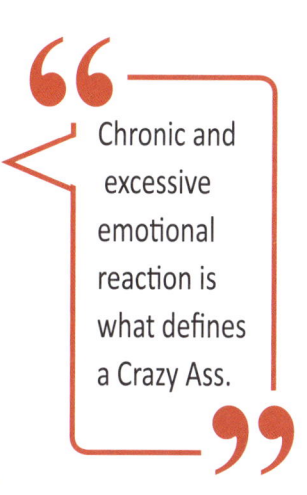

> Chronic and excessive emotional reaction is what defines a Crazy Ass.

    A word to you single people out there when it comes to detecting Crazy Ass in a person's character: *You date the act. You marry the re-act.* Anyone can act in a certain way…that's why it's called acting. What you want to look for is the *reaction* when life hits the fan. Reactions are hard to fake. What happens to their demeanor when the pressure is on or when things don't go according to plan?

DON'T BE AN ASS

What is their response when their computer crashes or a clerk shorts them on the correct amount of change? (I've also heard that a true test of one's character is how they handle untangling Christmas lights or assembling furniture from Ikea!) Does their crazy come spilling out or do they handle themselves with grace and poise? Oftentimes, Crazy Ass is really easy to spot from a mile away...if you have your eyes open and are looking. When you see a person react badly, don't make the mistake of thinking, "Oh! That's not who he *really* is!" or "She isn't normally like that!" Hello!! That's *exactly* who that person really is!

What Crazy Asses need more than anything else is a healthy dose of perspective. Believe me, the end of the world isn't upon us just because your husband didn't buy the brand of white bread that you normally get. The earth will not stop spinning on its axis over the fact that your wife overdrew the checking account. Armageddon is not imminent as a result of the smeared finger paint on the table and floor. There is no need to go on a tirade of biblical proportion making yourself upset and creating havoc for everyone close to you.

Instead of taking all form and manner of offense, rather than feeling forever upset and slighted, in lieu of living in an eternal state of hurt feelings, anger, and bereavement, verbally vomiting your emotions all over those around you, how about you take a step back and "check yourself before you wreck yourself"...or before you wreck the people closest to you. Try to evaluate your reactions to what's going on--is it worth a Mount Vesuvius response, or will a slow, quiet trickle do? Look in the mirror--is your crazy showing? Then you might want to tuck that back in.

 The truth is, most of you Crazy Ass people don't see or realize your berserk has snuck out and is laying on full display for the viewing pleasure of all. It is for this very reason you must allow others to speak into your life. Listen to what the people around you say in terms of your behavior. I know, I know...when someone tells you to calm down and get a grip, when they try to explain to you that your crazy isn't a reasonable response to a given situation, it only makes you more crazy! But they are saying it for your own good. The people who love and care about you are trying to help you be more effective in your relationships.

 Gain some insight into how your friends, family or coworkers pull off more subtle and subdued reactions to the highs and lows of life. How do they process things? What keeps them from freaking out when everything doesn't go according to plan? Learn from them.

DON'T BE AN ASS

I am always amazed that people get so overwrought by the normal things of life. Your in-laws irritate you that badly? Your kids drive you crazy when they just act like kids? Your spouse rubs you the wrong way when they do what they've always done? Work sometimes sucks and your boss makes you batty? Seriously?? That is all normal life. You are delusional if you think life on this fallen, sin-filled planet is supposed to be all rainbows and butterflies. You need to chill out. Take a deep breath and ask yourself: *In the course of a lifetime, what will it matter?* In the words of Aaron Rodgers: R-E-L-A-X! (Green Bay Packer fans will understand the reference. If you are not a Packer lover - well, it sucks to be you.) You'll be amazed at the improvement it will make in your relationships. You will benefit and everyone around you will appreciate the break from the drama and emotional bedlam that follows in the wake of a Crazy Ass.

> What Crazy Asses need more than anything is a healthy does of perspective.

Conclusion

Maybe you have seen a bit of yourself in these pages. If so, don't get angry. A book like this is intended to be a mirror. Mirrors are good things: They show us what we really look like. If we look like crap, the mirror will expose it so we can do something about it. Getting angry at the mirror would only be an exercise in futility.

Oftentimes, like in the case of the mirror, just being able to see and be aware is what makes all the difference. It is when we look and see we have egg on our face that we can wipe it off. It is when we see our hair is going wild that we can tame it with a comb. I know no one person is perfect. To be honest, I can see a bit of myself in some of these pages.

Be aware. Look in the mirror. Make some adjustments. Try to show more understanding towards others knowing that we all need as

DON'T BE AN ASS

much grace and understanding as others can give us while we struggle with our own versions of Assedness.

Try to be a bit less stubborn, a bit less lazy, a bit less arrogant, a bit less stupid, a bit less smart, a bit less egotistical, a bit less stingy, and a lot less critical.

In short… Don't Be an Ass.

More books by Mark Gungor:

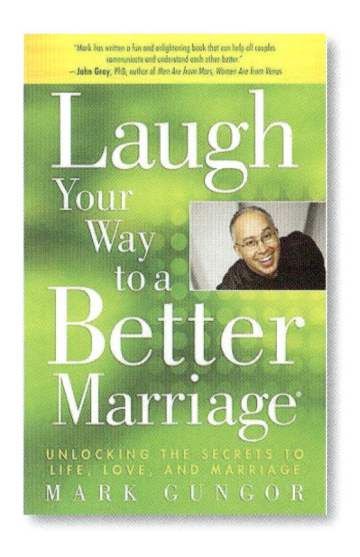

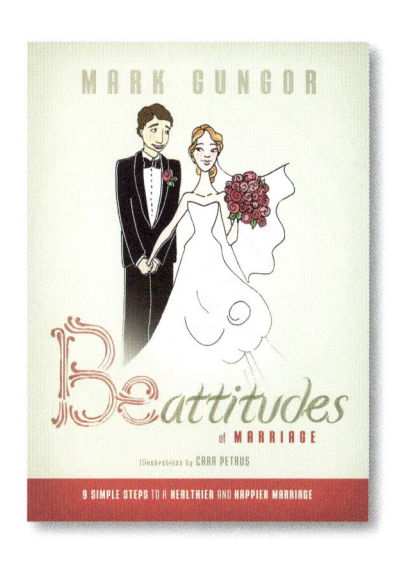

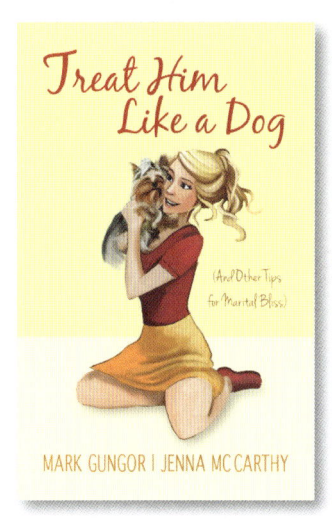

www.markgungor.com